The Only Way Out

is

The Only Way Out

is

a guide to moving forward
for single mothers

Laura Conner

Published by Master Press

© Copyright 2009 Master Press. All Rights Reserved

No part of this book may be reproduced, stored in a retrieval system, or transmitted in any form or by any means—electronic, mechanical, photocopy, recording, or otherwise—except for brief quotations for the purpose of review or comment, without the prior permission of the publisher.

Printed in the United States of America

Laura Conner
    The Only Way Out is In
Laura Conner
    ISBN# 978-0-9790296-3-9

Master Press
318 S.E. 4th Terrace
Cape Coral, Fl 33990

Visit us on the web at: www.master-press.com

Dedication

This book is dedicated with love and affection to Brian. You make Motherhood one of the greatest experiences of my life. It has been a privilege and an honor to call you my son.

My eternal thanks to God, our Creator, for His exquisite design of Woman. I am most grateful to discover and live out the wonderful facets that He has placed within me.

To single mothers, everywhere. May you look inside and uncover the DNA of your design as Woman and pass this Legacy of Greatness onto your children.

Content

Chapter 1   The Event 11

Chapter 2   The Prototype 19

Chapter 3   Fallout 29

Chapter 4   Seeking a Salve 37

Chapter 5   Who Do You Think You Are? 47

Chapter 6   What Do You See? 55

Chapter 7   Go Within or You'll Go Without .. 63

Chapter 8   The Unveiling 73

Chapter 9   More Revelation 83

Chapter 10   Practically Speaking 93

Introduction

Statistics say that today's divorce rate is between 50-60%. Add to that, unexpected pregnancies, broken relationships or the death of a mate, a great multitude of women find themselves in the throws of a life scenario in which they were never taught to function. Now they are expected to move their family forward into uncharted territory without a script! Because most single mothers are living in Survival Mode, many are totally unaware how their choices are making a tremendous and lasting impact on their children. The stark reality is that these precious, but desperate, women are shaping society's future generations! <u>The Only Way Out is In</u> gives these ladies the hope and tools they need for a successful family life. It encourages them in the greatest challenge of their life. <u>The Only Way Out is In</u> is the first book in a series for this much-neglected sector of the world's society living in quiet desperation.

The Event

"To love oneself is the beginning of a lifelong romance"
Oscar Wilde (1854-1900)

She comes to us in the opposite spirit and her greeting is one of peace; nothing lacking, nothing missing. Soundness, wholeness, and completeness are the gifts she brings with her. As she comes close enough to greet us face to face, a light shines forth from her eyes. It's a light of reflection and of deep calling unto deep. Looking into her eyes we see a reflection of... our Self; the template, prototype and original Divine design. She lives in us; she is us. At the very core of our existence, we are Woman.

It was supposed to be "happily ever after". After all, that's what we were promised from all those fairy tales we were introduced to as impressionable little girls. Some of us grew up seeing the video or reading the storybooks over and over again. We believed the stories and dreamed of the day when our prince would arrive. And we patiently waited for time to transform us from little girls to women because it was then that our prince would come and carry us away to our own world of storybook romance.

When "our day" finally arrived, we were filled with great joy and expectation of a bright and beautiful future. We dressed for the occasion, made eternal promises to each other and believed that our bliss would last for a lifetime. We moved forward into marriage and the future believing that our "happily ever after" had only just begun. But for some of us, a good many of us, the story had a very different ending from those we daydreamed about during childhood.

Today looks a whole lot different; our storybook romance went from daydream to bad dream and we awoke and asked, "What happened?" Our stories differ in the cast of characters, plot and ending, but they all share a common thread. It didn't turn out the way the storybook said it would. For some the story ended in a tragic and premature death. Others experienced some kind of separation or divorce. Even if separation or divorce was a welcomed thing for us it still wasn't part of our original dream. Now we find that we are alone, trying to find the answers for our selves and those who represent a love that was once fruitful ~ our children.

This place feels different, really different. Even our identity is obscured if only for a short time. Our place of existence is almost a paradox. We are no longer a maiden who bears her father's name, yet neither are we a wife bearing the name of her spouse. Some of us have chosen to keep a name our children have but no longer describe who we currently are, and the paradox continues. It's awkward, uncomfortable, unfamiliar and uncertain. It's a place we've not been before and it brings a lot of questions for which we are unsure of the answers.

> *Our story went from daydream to bad dream and we awoke and asked, "What happened?"*

It seems everyone wants to know why. Our friends, family, children, co-workers and even the casual curious, look to us for the answers, and if we had one we could understand, we'd give it. No one wants answers more than we do! We've laid awake at night rehearsing every scene a million times and tried to see if the story could have turned out differently. It never did. Even if we think we have a solid reason for What has happened, it's the Why that keeps peace of mind so elusive. Our head is swimming and our heart is fractured and remembering our name is a big achievement these days. And the biggest question we have is "Now what?"

This book is about you and me and millions of women just like us. We are the ones whose stories didn't end happily; they just ended. We make up a great majority of the population and we are one of the largest groups living at poverty level. We've stepped into a place that has required us to pick up the fragments of the family, become the leader and move everyone successfully forward into an unknown future. All this without a script! We are single mothers.

The weight of the world has seemingly been laid upon us and we wonder why our back and shoulders constantly ache. Insomnia has become an unwelcome friend because now we sleep with one eye open and our ears attuned to the slightest sounds of the night. Our newly acquired positioned also includes that of protector and while we may be fearful we would make a mother bear proud. The workday has increased to 24/7 and this we do without overtime, bonuses or holiday pay. Stress levels are off the chart and our "last nerve" is usually mangled by the time we get the kids to school and ourselves to work. We keep hearing the phrase, *"I'm so tired"*, and discover the voice that keeps repeating it is our own. Finally we come to the conclusion that those words are what now describe our very state of existence. Our financial situation suffers the most. We have worked two and three jobs to make ends meet. Child support sounds good in theory, but many women never see a dime even if the courts have ordered it. In reality it's still a fraction of provision when compared to having a whole additional income. We try to hold up under all the pressure but we break down. If we're smart we do this after the kids are asleep so they don't become more fearful. As hard as our life has become, we realize the most difficult task is to look into the eyes of our children. Seeing their pain, and hearing them cry from the depths of their soul is unbearable. Yet, we try to be strong and make life as normal as possible...whatever that is. I don't remember any book telling this story and this certainly isn't what I signed up for at the wedding ceremony. But it is, after all...my life.

Life has become chaotic at best and for the lucky ones, the chaos is short lived. These fortunate women have a group of loving people who have gathered around for support and encouragement, even help. Others have had to go it alone and the solitude feels like a never-ending black hole.

People look at us differently, mostly with judgment. Our married friends disappear because we are no longer a "couple". Perhaps they are afraid of their own marriage having a similar outcome, or the wife becomes afraid of losing her husband to the newly single. Whatever the reason, we feel the loss. Even the places we thought for sure we'd find support, we are surprised to see the reactions. Family members, co-workers and even those in our places of worship see us with a different view as if we're just *not quite right now*. Most are not honest enough to admit they have judged, labeled or stigmatize us but the unspoken is so loud it's deafening. How much more do we have to lose?

> *I'm not the woman who wants to prove I can do it all because now, I have to.*

How do I move forward into that for which I am unqualified? I'm not built for this. Oh sure, I may be strong and courageous, capable and intelligent, but this new position requires something more along the order of superwoman. I'm not the woman who wants to prove I can do it all because now I <u>have to</u>. I don't have a choice to turn back if I find it's just too hard. Funny how that phrase keeps running through my mind too... *"this is so hard"*. My life has shifted from "want to" to "have to" for the sake of those who depend on me. I've changed from Who I Am to Who I Have To Be and again feel a loss, but this time it's the greatest loss of all...me.

Would somebody please wake me up from this bad dream! How long is this going to last? Will life ever be different? What will become of my children? Will they turn out okay? Will we survive this? How much more do we have to suffer? When am I going to be happy again?

HOW DO I GET OUT OF THIS PLACE!

These are the questions we ask ourself while alone at night, hot tears streaming down our face, praying for sleep to rescue us from reality, if only for a few short hours.

Uncertain of our self and the road ahead, we begin to put one foot in front of the other and walk into the future. Inside we are fearful and trembling but outside we look together for the sake of our children and those who are watching. And yes, we are always mindful that they are watching. "Onward and upward" is a lofty goal and our real achievement is to make it to the end of the day in one piece. We're doing the best we can; some have done better than others. At this stage of the game when we're trying to "hold it all together" we don't yet understand that

>...the only way out is in.

The Prototype

> *"How wrong it is for a woman to expect the man to build the world she wants, rather than to create it herself."*
> Anais Nin (1903-1977)

"To live"..." to breathe"..."life"..."enlivening"..."living one"..."mother". These are the words that describe her. We are acquainted with her by name, but her reputation is known virtually by every person who has ever lived. She was the prototype for woman and her name is Eve. We don't really know who she was; we just know what she did. To this day she has never lived it down. It's one thing when we make a mistake that affects us personally or those in our family, but it's a whole different story when our actions affect the entire human race. What a reputation to be known for, to have to live with, even after thousands of years have past!

Looking at all the words that describe her, we see an immediate contradiction. If she was the woman of "life" and the "living one", how is it that she acted in a way that brought about such death and destruction? I've heard Eve spoken of many times...mostly with disdain. Somehow there had to be more to the story. While most focused on the What, I began to focus on the Why and the Who. It was time to really become acquainted with her myself. In doing so, I was hoping to gain an understanding of her contradiction. Maybe it would help to clear up my own. My discovery paid off with an incredible revelation. Not only is she the prototype of Woman, she is also the answer for women. If we have the courage to be honest and conscious, we'll see that the apple hasn't fallen far from the tree...so to speak!

Eve was unique. The historical account of her life is interesting. I found her in the creation story of Genesis; she's alluded to in the very first chapter. It was here that Her Creator decreed the mission statement of her life. It was the very same one given to Adam (Man). "Be productive, increase, subdue the earth and rule over the other species of creation."[1] Sounds like the job description of a Chief Executive Officer! She is described in more detail in the second chapter of the same book. It is here that her uniqueness is revealed. Looking carefully at the account of Eve, we see that she is different from all the other creation, Adam included. The creation account tells us that every living creature, Man included, was formed from the dust of the ground. But not Eve! She was created from something different...a part of Man. She was also the "finishing touch" of creation...the last formation by the Creator. Most important was the fact that she was able to do something that no other part of creation was capable of doing.

Eve was able to do what her Creator had done; she was able to create a being ~ her children ~ in the image of God. Woman was a masterpiece!

Talk about a place of power and authority! She never had to "climb the ladder"; she was already positioned at the top! Woman, producer, subduer, ruler, living one and distinctly hers alone ~ creator. How would you like to list those attributes on your resume? What if your life was defined and described by these very same words? This is the real Eve that doesn't get much press. But she is the one whom all women aspire to be like. She's not only the woman that "has it all"; she's the woman that is it all! The good news for you and me is that Eve is our prototype; the mold, pattern, example for who we are too. We are her descendants and somewhere within, our DNA carries the imprint of her same greatness.

> *We are her descendants and somewhere within, our DNA carries the imprint of her same greatness.*

Enter the contradiction. If Eve was so powerful, how could she have done the What? Have you ever asked yourself the same question?

Why did I do that?...What was I thinking?... How could I have been so foolish?

The questioning is endless and haunting. But that's as far as it goes, just questioning. Most of us don't look for the answers because we're afraid of what we'll find. Our fear keeps us stuck, trapped, hindered; it keeps us from moving forward. If we look to Eve, we'll recognize ourselves.

The saying is that good news travels fast, bad news travels faster. Eve's news has traveled the longest. The quick read is that Eve ate the forbidden fruit, gave it to Adam and is responsible for the fall of mankind. Period, end of story. That synopsis is nice and tidy and has led to an inferior perception of woman that has simmered on the back burner of her unconscious thinking. It's here that I began to ask "why". Eve tells us the story herself in the same book of Genesis, chapter 3.

After the devastating Event, the Designer of the product wanted to see why it malfunctioned. This isn't what He had in mind while He was creating woman, but something went wrong, very wrong. The Creator asked the woman, "What is this you have done?"[2] I don't think He was angry, I think He wanted her to engage in self-awareness. Eve, at this point, had already tried to hide herself with fig leaves. Don't we do the same? Only we don't use fig leaves, we use excuses. These excuses are very convenient because they keep us from the answers ~ the very thing that will set us free. Eve responds to her Creator by saying, "The serpent deceived me and I ate."[3] To many, it sounds like blame shifting and a really good excuse. However, Eve was telling the truth; she was deceived. To be deceived means, "to ensnare, to cheat, to be false to, to cause to accept as true or valid what is false or invalid, to fail to fulfill".[4] The serpent told her that if she ate the fruit it would make her wise like her Creator. Because Eve used the word "deceived" she knew that took the bait, believed the lie. It was already declared in the first chapter of Genesis that she was made in the image of her Creator who obviously is unfathomably wise. Some in the telling of Eve's story have also discovered this fact and relayed it. Somehow, I wasn't satisfied to stop with this answer because once again it leads to the convenience of women feeling inferior by virtue of gender. I began to dig deeper.

The answer was obvious and familiar. I didn't find it when I looked at Eve; I found it when I looked at Man. Before the creation of Eve, Adam was functioning at his full capacity. Remember, they both had the same mission statement. In the second chapter of Genesis, it says that the Creator formed every beast of the field and every bird of the air and brought them to Adam, to see what he would name them. "And whatever Adam called each living creature, that was its name."[5] Can you imagine how long that must have taken? Every animal, every bird, every living creature that was made had to be named. The number of creatures was staggering, yet Adam had the ability to name every single one! Adam was operating in the capacity of co-creator. The Creator designed and Man declared. I find it interesting that the Creator allowed Adam to declare (name) His last creation. It says that "...He made [into] a woman, and He brought her to the man."[6] Adam called her Woman, and then later named her Eve. Being made in the image of the Creator, he had a vein of access to that unfathomable wisdom. Why the focus on Adam? Because his life shows us the key to why Eve was ensnared.

Eve stated with her own words that she was deceived. What was it that allowed her to be cheated? Why wasn't Adam the target of the serpent? Here's the revelation that reveals her actions. Unlike Adam, Eve, up to this point, had not **experienced** the capacity of the greatness that lie within her! Because she had not experienced her greatness or displayed her own access to unfathomable wisdom, Eve "failed to fulfill" (was deceived). The serpent wouldn't go to Adam because Adam knew who he was. He would have looked at the serpent and said, "Wise like God? I already am! If your memory serves you correctly, please recall that I named all of the living creatures and that would include you!" There's more to Adam's story and his downfall, but that's not our focus.

I propose it was the *failure to believe who she really was on the inside* that caused her to fail on the outside. Eve came into agreement with a lie about who she was. Because she had no "work experience", no recent opportunity to display her greatness, she doubted her true self. Instead of remembering her mission statement and looking inside at her design, Eve allowed an outside source to define her. Haven't we done the same thing? Haven't we allowed our circumstances and the Events in life tell us who we are? *You're divorced...you're a widow...you're a struggling single mom...you're alone...you're poor...you don't fit in now...you're not pretty enough...you're not good enough...you're not smart enough...* and the descriptions are endless. If we're honest with ourselves we'll agree that we, like Eve, have come into agreement with a lie about our true self. The resulting consequences of the What have traveled all through history.

> *I propose it was the failure to believe who she really was on the inside that caused her to fail on the outside.*

The Designer looked at Eve with what I believe to be great compassion. Although she was created in His image, He knew the great power of the other element ~ human nature. He told her that her desire (longing, craving) would be for her husband and that he (her husband) would rule (have dominion) over her.[7] This wasn't a punishment the Creator was administering. When I took a closer look at the human element I saw something interesting. The Creator was telling Eve what her actions had *set up* in her life. Put yourself in Eve's place. Not only did she make a grave mistake, she engaged her husband in the event. There's enough guilt when you make a mistake that affects you personally, but it becomes greatly multiplied when it involves someone you love. That guilt would cause Eve to always "desire" her husband's approval, affirmation, validation, and acceptance. Until this point in time, the humans ruled over the creation only, but now Man would "rule" over woman because she would feel inferior due to the What.

Look around and see the same pattern in women today. In some cultures it's very obvious, in others it may be hidden but still present. Women look to fathers, brothers, boyfriends, husbands for validation, affirmation, etc. If you give that kind of power to someone, they rule over you. If you're quiet enough to hear the still small voice of your heart speak, you may discover that a part of Eve lives in you too.

Take heart, dear friend, and remember. We as women were fashioned after an incredible prototype and her DNA of greatness is very much present within us. The answers for the issues of women today don't come from empty religion, public policy, culture or Man...they come from within.

Endnotes

1. Genesis 1:28
2. Genesis 3:13
3. ibid
4. Merriam Webster Online Dictionary, http://www.merriam-webster.com/, (accessed March 2009)
5. Genesis 2:19
6. Genesis 2:22
7. Genesis 3:16

> note: All endnote references are utilized with the author's license to paraphrase. You are encouraged to research the above references for your own study purposes.

Fallout

"If you are going through hell, keep going."
Sir Winston Churchill (1874-1965)

(Author's note: The names and actual events of the persons revealed in this chapter have been changed in part to protect their identity and privacy.)

And here we are...after the fallout. As best we can we're trying to "get on with our lives". Although we're not sure how we are supposed to do this we determine that we're going to just "move on". Our children need us to, our family wants us to, and in reality we know we have to. We convince our self that *I'm okay now, the kids will be just fine, and I'm really over what has happened.* We move forward into tomorrow not realizing that we smell like smoke, walk with a limp and our vision has been tainted. One cannot go through a life-altering event and not come out unaffected. We're in denial if we believe we can. We must process the situation and walk through a period of healing. But we're so busy now and our focus is on everything and everyone else but us. Who has the time? And besides, we're tired of hurting. It's easier to ignore than to inquire. We may self-deceive by our chosen ignorance but those around us are only too aware of our state of being.

Soundness, wholeness, and completeness are the gifts she brings with her.

She was one brave lady. It's not because she had been a single mom raising three children for the last 16 years. Kate revealed her courage by bearing her soul before a group of four hundred people. She was seeking an answer to a temporary situation but came away with the key that would change her life forever. Kate had been on the move ever since her divorce. She had relocated numerous times from one city to the next while convincing herself that she was being Divinely led. In her mind she even created situations that validated her irrational thought process. But today was the day for an appointment with truth, and she was desperate enough to hear it.

The leaders of the conference allowed for a question and answer segment in their schedule. So much information had been given and here was an opportunity for the crowd to process what they had heard. With great eagerness Kate was the first to stand and pose her question. It didn't have any relation to what we had heard for the last two days and seemed out of place. "Could you tell me how I can gain some stability and permanence in my life?" It really was the wrong question for this type of conference but fortunately for Kate, she asked the wrong question to the right leaders. Seasoned in interpersonal relationships, the keynote speakers immediately discerned Kate's present state of being; her brokenness was obvious. With great compassion and wisdom they began to gently but intently probe with a series of questions to bring her into a state of self-awareness. When she "came to" her moment of truth, Kate had to admit to herself that for the last decade and a half she had been running from the pain of her past.

Their life together was storybook romance. She truly had enjoyed a match made in heaven with the man of her dreams. Sara and Tim, married for seventeen years, were still very much in love and in the midst of living happily ever after... until.

It was business as usual that day and everyone was in the midst of their morning routine. Tim was out for his early morning jog, the kids were deciding on what to have for breakfast and Sara was getting ready for work. In an instant, their lives would be forever changed. The phone rang and Sara thought it was probably one of the kids from school calling, again. But this time it wasn't a schoolmate; it was a police officer. Sara sunk into a chair as she heard the news that her prince, her best friend, the man that she was so desperately in love with, was hit by a car and killed while on his daily run. Immediately, she was paralyzed and time stood still as Sara felt a part of her die too.

I can't feel that! No matter how hard I pinch myself, there's no feeling. Is this what it's like to feel "numb"? Everything around me seems so surreal as if I'm watching a movie. Maybe I'm dead, but I can feel my heavy chest rising and falling. It's the only thing I can feel.

> *One cannot go through a life-altering event and not come out unaffected.*

The next few days, weeks and months would become a journey through great sorrow and darkness. At times Sara thought she would never make it through and wished she didn't have to try. She had no choice; she had to keep going for the sake of her children. Years later, she's still moving forward and although Sara is functioning on the outside, she's unaware that she's still not fully alive.

Stacey had a lot on the ball ~ bright, articulate and she possessed a great spirit of independence.

She was a born leader; great problem solver and her children adored her. Stacey was on the road to recovering from another divorce and life seemed to be smiling upon her with favor. Today she finds herself on the brink of disaster and instead of enjoying life she finds it unraveling. She's so busy trying to keep her head above water she doesn't stop and look at what's really going on around her. Stacey has repeated the cycle, the pattern, her place of familiarity. She goes around the circle again; another relationship with the same man (just a different name), financial ruin, drama and crisis. Using blame to explain her situation, Stacey is unaware that she herself has re-created her life circumstances all over again.

    She just couldn't take it anymore. Krista's life had been one problem after the other. Her day wasn't normal unless something went wrong... it always did. She came to expect the worst and never received less. Her friends were few and far between; they couldn't continue to endure the negativity and victim mentality. Even her co-workers had heard enough of the constant barrage of complaining and self-flagellation and avoided her like the plague. She was the "dark cloud" in the office.
    Krista always made the wrong decisions for herself and those around her ~ the children. She endured many years in a drug-filled marriage. She

married a man with a bad habit. It took its toll on the family and the destruction continued even after the marriage had ended. Her children were greatly affected and followed the imprint of drug addiction in their own lives. Life was one big crisis for Krista with no hope of ever getting better. She found herself at wit's end and her young son found her on the floor.

She had worked so hard all of her life. Erica was a career woman who was one of the very best in her field. Many people admired her ability and accomplishments. She was the "go to" girl who had the answers for those who had the questions. By outward observation one would think she had a great life and would enjoy an easy retirement. But behind the scenes no one knew that she was near financial ruin.

Erica's story ended in divorce but not before she and her husband brought four children into the picture. When the family dissolved Erica put her shoulder to the grind and became a great provider for her kids. She was always there and the children knew they could count on her...and they did.

The children grew up and began their walk into adulthood. But the divorce took its toll on two of the four and Erica was there once again for stability. Though Erica thought she was being a "good mom" she never realized that her actions were driven by guilt that her suffering children would use against her. The support continued in a monetary vein for way too long. Now everything is gone, savings, investments and even her retirement fund. The only retirement that Erica is presently looking forward to is a cemetery plot.

Do any of these stories sound familiar? Perhaps you can think of a friend who is living in a similar circumstance you just read about. Or, just maybe, you were able to identify... yourself. It's time to be honest with ourselves and realize that we cannot go through a life-altering event and not come out unaffected. Something will be formed in our thinking, fueled by our buried emotions that will now direct the course of our life and that of our children. Without going through a time of healing, we will develop judgments, mind-sets, misperceptions and self-limitations, to name a few! It's one thing if, we alone, were the only ones directed by the effects of the fallout, but make no mistake. Your children will suffer even more. They've had to endure the break up of the family and look to you for their stability. Can you give it out of your brokenness? How can you give comfort when you're in turmoil? What about reassurance when you're insecure? Is it possible to provide a place of stability when you're still in a place of reacting to the Event after all these years? You cannot give what you don't have! But on the flip side of that thought is that you *will give what you do have!* What are you giving your children? There's a saying that goes like this,

> "The fathers (parents) have eaten sour grapes…
> the children's teeth are set on edge."

Look around you ~ it's everywhere! But where we don't want it is in *your* home, *your* life and the lives of *your* children. You, yourself, have the power to change it, turn it around. Only **you** are the one to change the imprint made upon your life and your children's. And the easiest way to do it is...go within.

4
Seeking a Salve

"Believe in yourself! Have faith in your abilities! Without a humble but reasonable confidence in your own powers you cannot be successful or happy."
Norman Vincent Peale (1898 - 1993)

It's been a few months since the Event took place in our lives and some of the dust has now begun to settle. We're trying to move forward the best we can though life has seemingly shifted into "warp speed". Our schedule is now consumed with what I call Have To. Before the Event, our life had some combination of Have To/ Want To. In the past we were able to defer some of the Have To, to our spouse. *Could you please pick up Joey from baseball practice, I have to get Susie to her dental appointment? I'm meeting the girls for coffee after work. Can you start dinner?* With another adult in the picture we were able to have a more balanced life. Going solo changes the picture drastically.

Everyone's itinerary is different but they all encompass some involvement with what seems like the literal Three Ring Circus ~ Work, Kids, Home. There's always some kind of activity happening in each of the rings simultaneously. If by chance there is a moment of silence in one of the rings, you can be sure that something or someone will quickly jump into the ring to assure that you don't get a break! Trying to keep up with the children's schedules alone can be compared to herding baby ducks! How do you stay on top of school work, science projects, band practice/concerts, sports activities, ballet lessons, painting class, orthodontic appointments, sleep-overs, field trips, parental visitation? Of course it can look easy as it's written out so precisely on the calendar but living it is very different! The calendar says that Tim's Science Fair is at 7:00pm tomorrow evening, but it's 10:00 o'clock the night before and we're in the car on our way to the store because he forgot something for his project that *the teacher says we must have [it]!* There's always something to disrupt our schedule, which in turn disrupts what little peace we have.

Our Have To becomes all consuming and we wonder where Want To went and if it's ever coming back. We feel like Have To has completely taken over our life and that our existence is solely to care for those we are responsible for. The balance of Want To/Have To has now become the conflict of Don't Want To/Have To. We're so busy taking care of everyone else; we don't have time to even think about taking care of our self. Place that conflict next to the Who I Am/Who I Have To Be issue and angry sparks are sure to fly! But we're trying to "let the dust settle" and so our highly charged emotion turns into quiet desperation. We continue to move forward, missing our life and still very much broken. At this point we become most vulnerable.

> *The balance of Want To/Have To has now become the conflict of Don't Want To/Have To.*

The pace of Warp Speed quickly becomes overwhelming and along the way we've given out so many pieces of our self there's almost nothing left. Our spirit inspires us to move ahead for the sake of the children, our body is always running on fumes and hovers just above total exhaustion. But it's our soul ~ our mind, will and emotions ~ that we must protect from vulnerability.

It's been such a long time since we've felt anything good. Deep within our soul thirsts and it feels like we've been walking the Sahara desert with no water in sight. We long for just one cool drop of moisture to refresh us if only for a moment. Our soul is the place where our brokenness lives and houses all the self-talk.

I can't take much more of this...I'm so lonely... How come I never get to do what I want anymore? ... Life isn't fair...What did I do to deserve this? ...I don't know how much longer I can go on.

Our self-talk fuels our vulnerability and we hear the deceiving whisper of the serpent tell us that mirage ahead is really an oasis. Too many of us have taken the bait, believed the lie, became deceived. Deception comes in all kinds of disguises and it's hard to discern its falsehood when your soul is really thirsty, tired and broken. Afar off, the oasis looks enticing and exciting. After a long walk in the hot desert our vision is askew and we think the water ahead will refresh us. To satisfy the thirsting of our soul and the pain in our heart, we plunge right in.

"You know, it's been such a long week and I deserve a break. I think I'll stop buy the store after work and get a bottle of wine; that should relax me. Besides, I don't really drink, but hey, I'm an adult now and I'm in charge and I can do whatever I want. And if it helps me forget about my troubles for a little while, more power to me."

"I never noticed before how handsome Ron is! We've worked together for over three years, how did I ever overlook him? He's got a great position with the company, has never been married and really has some class and style. I've heard that he drinks a little and has a real eye for the ladies, but I don't think he'd be unfaithful if we ever got together. It may be time to get back into the dating game and I think I've found an opportunity right in front of me. I'm tired of being alone."

"These credit cards are sure adding up! I know I'm getting behind in my bills but you know, shopping is the only thing I do for me and because I work so hard, I deserve it! I'll find a way to pay these credit cards off somehow."

It's not till later, and sometimes much later, that we discover the water was poisonous.

Vulnerability and self-talk ~ the wrong kind, can really put us in a position to make some bad choices. Maybe even some choices we wouldn't have made if we weren't so vulnerable. The problem is that most women don't realize what kind of state they are really in. They're too busy trying to keep up with the Three Ring Circus while convincing themselves and those around them that "everything's just fine". They lose objectivity as they lose their self.

> A light shines forth from her eyes.
> It's a light of reflection and of deep calling unto deep.

The typical single mom is tired ~no, exhausted, lonely, overwhelmed, overburdened and barely keeping her head above water financially while being pulled in many different directions at the same time! She would welcome relief from somewhere, which quickly turns into ANYWHERE when the desperation inside her grows to the tipping point. This is where she is most vulnerable and some have even convinced themselves that poison doesn't really taste that bad!

Enter the serpent. (Remember our prototype, Eve?) What really is the serpent? In a nutshell, It's an opportunity of deception, clothed in false truth that leads to our destruction. It provides us with an occasion to " be ensnared" and to "fail to fulfill" while trying to convince us that what is before us will quench our thirst. The template is the same... contemplate something that looks pleasant, justify your need for it, engage yourself with it, reap the inevitable destruction. The pattern has been around for thousands of years and is obviously still quite effective. The serpent has mastered the skills of observation and impeccable timing. Its hearing is acute and patience is Its strong suit. The serpent knows when to present us with an occasion because It waits for our self-talk to come through our speech as an invitation for conversation.

"IT'S JUST ONE LITTLE DRINK, THAT'S ALL. IT WILL HELP YOU UNWIND AND RELAX. WOULDN'T IT BE GREAT TO FORGET ALL YOUR TROUBLES FOR JUST A FEW MINUTES? IT'S NO BIG DEAL. YOU CAN HANDLE IT."

"YOU SURE ARE LONELY. IT'S BEEN SUCH A LONG TIME SINCE ANYONE HAS PAID ANY ATTENTION TO YOU. WOULDN'T IT FEEL GREAT TO HAVE ROMANCE BACK IN YOUR

LIFE? DON'T YOU WANT SOMEONE TO JUST HOLD YOU AGAIN? DON'T WORRY; RON WILL CHANGE AFTER YOU'RE MARRIED. BESIDES, YOU NEED A MAN TO TAKE CARE OF YOU AND THE KIDS."

"YOU WORK SO HARD. DON'T YOU DESERVE A LITTLE SOMETHING FOR YOUR SELF? JUST PUT IT ON THE CREDIT CARD AND WORRY ABOUT IT LATER. YOU GIVE TO EVERYBODY ELSE, IT'S TIME YOU GIVE TO YOU

It's one thing to fall for deception because we've been blindsided but it's a whole different story when we get closer to the oasis, notice something odd about the water and still drink it!

When you saw a slimy film floating on the top or noticed a funny smell as you drew closer, it would have been easy to detect that the oasis may contain bad water. But when it's sparkling blue and looks crystal clear we assume it's fine drink. We don't bother to "test the water". In either case we begin to justify and the greater the thirst, the more we tell our self

> *It's an opportunity of deception, clothed in false truth that leads to our destruction. It provides us with an occasion to "be ensnared" and to "fail to fulfill".*

SEEKING A SALVE • 43

that the water really is okay! Here's something **vital** we must learn:

If justification is the fuel our self-talk uses to propel us forward, we are going down the wrong road.

Why? Because we are taking the bait, believing the lie, becoming deceived! Now we become "snake handlers" and convince ourselves that *"I can handle this",* while refusing to understand that inevitably we will be bit.

So *what's the big deal?* you may ask yourself (another sign of justification). The most important consideration is the fact that **you are not alone in the fallout.** The destruction will make a great impact on your children as well. Do they deserve more of the same or will you justify what happens to them also? Remember, you are **imprinting** on their life! What exactly does that mean? It means, "To fix indelibly or permanently (as on the memory)."[1] The definition speaks volumes itself.

Another consideration is you, yourself! Do you want to compromise the greatness of who you are, your original DNA imprint, your authentic self? Is it really worth it in exchange for a drink of water that will never quench your thirst and lead you in search of another oasis? Your search will be endless until you realize that the only water that will ever satisfy you comes from...within.

Endnotes

1. Merriam Webster Online Dictionary, http://www.m-w.com/, (accessed April 2009)

5
Who Do You Think You Are?

"I am still determined to be cheerful and happy, in whatever situation I may be; for I have also learned from experience that the greater part of our happiness or misery depends upon our dispositions, and not upon our circumstances."
Martha Washington ~ wife of George Washington
1759 (1732 - 1802)

"How does the sun come up so quickly? Can't it wait a little while longer? Do I really have to face another day? I'm so tired and I don't know if I have it in me to keep going. I know the kids need me to be there for them but who's there for me? I don't know if I have anything left to give...not even another breath."

The sound of that alarm clock going off can seem like the worst noise we've ever heard. It signals that we must face our life again and the endless struggle to make it through another day. It reminds us we have no choice to turn it off, go back to sleep and pretend this is all a bad dream.

Instead it awakens us to the reality that yes, this really is happening to us and we may not know what to do to make it better.

Some single moms have tried various things to make life better; take some of the pressure off. Many have gone back to school, gotten a college degree and started a new career or furthered their existing one. Others have used their creativity and started a business with one simple thought. And there are also those moms who have taken what resources they have and multiplied them through investments. These ladies have utilized the talents and abilities they possess to move them forward into a better financial situation for their families. They have greatly reduced the pressure of "making ends meet"...one of the biggest stressors of all.

Unfortunately, not all mothers have been as successful and we hear about their tragic stories on the news. The pressure became too great and they snapped under the weight of it all. Life was more than they could handle and so they ended it for themselves and/or their children. Our hearts grieve for their loss and although we may not be able to understand what they did, we can identify with what they felt.

I believe that somewhere in the midst of these scenarios lie the majority of single mothers. They are the women who live in what I call "survival mode". They are doing the best they can with what they have and are desperately trying to make a normal life for themselves and their loved ones. When the alarm goes off they get out of bed, put one foot in front of the other and bravely face another day. Their lives are motivated by Have To. But Survival Mode becomes very wearing and makes one even more vulnerable to drinking poisonous water. It may not make the evening news but it can sure lead to a lot of destruction.

Being a single mother feels like living in a pressure cooker. It's hot, confining and full of pressure! There's a small release valve on the top of the pot that allows the pressure to be released when the contents have finished cooking. But most mothers don't know when their life circumstances are going to change and some have tried to find the release valve that will give them some sort of relief ~ even if it is just temporary. And so they "pick their poison" not knowing, or even more true, not wanting to know what the outcome will be so long as some of the pressure is off.

These are the ones who try their luck at being "snake handlers". Justification and rationalization are their best allies for getting involved in something that will bring devastation, ultimately leading to more grief, sorrow and brokenness. They move ahead, confident and assured that they have found something to eliminate some of the pressure; relieve some of the stress. At last, relief is in sight! Or is it, really? Your friends of justification and rationalization can keep you comfortably deceived, but they can't keep you from being bit.

Some time goes by and they begin to notice things they didn't see in the beginning. With a rapid response, the allies come to the rescue and save them from the truth, which allows them to keep moving in the wrong direction. They continue on the pathway paved with self-deception ignoring the large potholes and road signs warning of the dangers ahead. The needs on the inside are greater than the dangers on the outside and so they move ahead into the Destruction Zone. It's here where crisis calls out and the alarm goes off screaming a wake up call.

> *Looking into her eyes we see a reflection of...our self; the template, prototype and original divine Design.*

"How can this be happening? How can they take my kids from me? They have no right to do this! They're wrong... all of them! I am not an unfit mother! I love my kids! I just need a little drink to help me get through the day. I can quit any time I want! I don't have a drinking problem! So what if I lost my job and the kids have missed a few meals. This happens to people all the time. It's that teacher's fault! She accused me of being drunk at the parent/teacher conference. What does she know? This is her fault! She called the social worker and made up lies about me, and she got the kids to lie

about me too! How could she turn my kids against me? What kind of person does that? They don't know what I have to go through ~ how hard my life is! I just need a little something to help me get through this. Give me back my kids!"

"Oh my God, NO! It can't be! It just can't! I'm pregnant? Both tests confirm it's true! How did this happen when I've been on the pill? What am I going to do? I'm 38 years old and I didn't want any more kids! I can't even afford the ones I already have! And how do I tell them? How do I tell my parents? Oh no, Oh no. Please don't let this be true, it just can't be. That loser, Ron! I broke it off with him three weeks ago because I found out he was cheating on me! And now I'm pregnant with his baby? My friends and co-workers warned me about him, but I wouldn't listen. I thought I could change him! The worst part is, I had a funny feeling about him from the very start. What am I going to do now!?"

> *The needs on the inside are greater than the dangers on the outside and so they move ahead into the Destruction Zone.*

"I can't believe what I'm reading! The mortgage company is sending me a notice of foreclosure? But I've been talking to the people at that

company and told them that I was having a hard time financially. They told me nine months ago that they would work with me. It sure doesn't look like they're working very hard! I told them that my credit card bills were really piling up and that I needed to take money out of the house to pay for them. I did pay them off, but they have large balances again. They don't understand that I need things for the kids and for myself. I can't pay everything at once! What do they expect? I'm not made of money! Now they want to turn my family out on the street! Why are they doing this to me?"

My sister, my friend...where are you? Are you walking the Sahara with an unquenchable thirst looking for an oasis...that place you hope will refresh and satisfy?

Maybe you have grown extremely weary and hopelessness continuously haunts you while whispering, "There's no way out." Have you hit the Destruction Zone and are you becoming intimately acquainted with drama and crisis? Where are you my sister, my friend...where are you? The question isn't being asked in reference to geographical location. It's meant to bring you

> *Your friends of justification and rationalization can keep you comfortably deceived, but they can't keep you from being bit.*

into the present moment and reveal your level of consciousness. Are you fully awakened to what is happening around you and where your path is taking you? Can you clearly see where you are headed and what kind of journey your children will experience as they follow you? Are you aware of how your choices are affecting their lives and leaving an indelible imprint? Are you fully present in this moment ~ free of deception, false beliefs and mindsets that come to rob you of your greatness, your true self? Or are you in the midst of fallout where crisis has sounded the alarm and you sit on the ash-heap of more brokenness, heartache and devastation? There's a whole gamut of places in between but what's most important is that you can truthfully answer the question,

WHERE ARE YOU?

If we don't know where we are or chose to remain in self-deception or brokenness, our moving forward will only be in a circle and we are destined to repeat more of the same.

Many times, the circumstances of life bring the Aha! moment to people. I'm asking you to give yourself a gift, an opportunity for that moment to happen now.

Only when we choose to be fully conscious and aware can we break out of the cycle and move towards the person we were created to be, living the life we were meant to live. This results in our children having the chance to achieve the highest potential of all that they are meant to be also.

> *Only when we choose to be fully conscious and aware can we break out of the cycle and move towards the person we were created to be.*

It's time to stop and discover your level of consciousness and your location. It's time to locate the degree of fullness you are walking in. It's time to remember that your DNA as a woman is filled with greatness. It's time to become fully alive. It's time to realize that we've wasted too much time looking for something "out there" and that we ourselves possess all that we are looking for. It's been there all along...inside.

6
What Do You See?

"I discovered I always have choices, and sometimes it's only a choice of attitude."
Judith M. Knowlton

"Location, location, location." One of the utmost important things to consider when purchasing any piece of property is where it is physically located. Location alone can make a big difference in the value of the building. A beautiful, custom-built home with all the latest amenities will sell for a much higher price if it's situated on a beachfront or golf course rather than backing up to the city dump. Location alone can determine value, desirability and marketability.

Have you ever seen someone you know go through a difficulty and say to yourself, "She's in a bad place"? What did you observe that made you think so? Was it something in her behavior, her attitude, countenance or perhaps her speech that led you to come to such a conclusion? What caused you to judge her location as "bad"?

Have you ever said that about... your self? Did you find your location by answering the question, "Where Are You"? Without a doubt, it's a very tough question to answer because it requires a lot of courage and complete honesty. It also requires something more...

"Where am I? I'll tell you where I am! I'm in this really hard place and so are my kids because He put us here!"

Many single mothers are still so focused on the "Why" (The Event) that they don't know, or refuse to see, the "Where" ~ location. Discovering our location requires courage and honesty, but it also requires letting go of blame. Consider this: Suppose you were in a single-engine plane that crashed in a forest. You survive the crash and radio for help. You are able to speak to the leader of the Search and Rescue team and he assures you they are ready to save you. When he asks for your location, all you do is talk about the crash, rehearsing what happened over and over. He interrupts your storytelling to once again refocus you on your location, but to no avail. Once more, you have to relay the story of your trauma. What are the chances of you fully surviving if you don't stop talking about the crash and start looking at where you are? Your chances of rescue are slim to none.

Am I trying to minimize what happened in your life that caused or contributed to you being in this Hard Place? No, of course not. We've all had our own story of grief and sorrow. What I am trying to get you to do is to refocus from Capitalize to Minimize. YES, it was a terrible event. YES, it broke

> *Discovering our location requires courage and honesty, but it also requires letting go of blame.*

your heart and hurt your children. YES, it left you in this really tough place in life. No one will argue that you've had trauma, pain and find yourself in a place that wasn't a part of your dreams for the future. But if you choose not to stop and look at where you currently are, you can't ever see how to move forward into something different. Life will never change.

I experienced my own Event ~ a divorce. Because I wanted the divorce, the ending of my marriage was a relief for me. The hardest part was how it affected my son. But it was something that happened years later that made me stop and locate myself. For a long time after this particular Event, I kept focusing on what had happened. Finally, I changed my focus from It to Me. It was then that I began to make progress.

Again, if you choose not to stop and look at where you currently are, you can't ever see how to move forward into something different. Life will never change. The level of pain was so great, I realized I needed help to sort it all out and return to a place of wholeness. Fortunately, I had some incredible friends who were well versed and experienced in inner healing. Applying their wisdom and tools, along with other materials I discovered, propelled me into a level of peace, joy and contentment I had never before experienced. Little did I know that while engaged in this process of wholeness, I would also discover the Greatness imprinted in my DNA, my authentic self, the real me! It was a delightful bonus!

She lives in us; she is us.

Locating yourself requires self-examination and self-awareness. It demands that we separate ourselves from how we are functioning on the outside to focusing on how we are feeling on the inside. It's the first step to the healing process. Some single moms have closed the door to their heart because the pain is just too great and decided that not feeling at all is a better option. The problem with that decision is the consequence of not being able to fully give or receive the precious love our children need and have to offer. We must honestly evaluate what effects The Event have imprinted on our life. We may be fooled into thinking that because we are functioning well on the outside that we are doing just fine on the inside. *But remember, one cannot go through a life-altering change and not come out unaffected.* At minimum you will come away with some misperception (probably about yourself!), a false belief (again, about yourself and/or men, relationships, life, etc) or some subtle change in your thinking that will be self-limiting. If you're having a hard time with this process, enlist the help of a trusted, loving friend who can objectively see what you may not be able to see. But you must be willing to hear the truth. Don't ask for help and then become upset with what you hear. Remember, truth has the ability to free us. We don't want our greatness to be diminished and then walk through life with pieces of the fallout still impacting our life and our children. We deserve better!

Another important dimension to focus on is forgiveness. Unforgiveness can single-handedly chain us to the Event and keep us from ever moving anywhere except in a circle. It allows our former mate to control us and stay connected to us, which attracts the very same thing to us! It's also deadly to our children because it can leave a toxic imprint on their lives. A personal friend relayed the story of his parents' divorce when he was a child. His father had left the family when he was just a young boy, which left the family devastated. Although abandonment issues impacted him with his dad, he confessed feelings of hatred toward his mother. All his growing up years after his father had left; he had to listen to his mother spew her bitterness about the Event. The best policy is to never speak poorly about the former mate. We must support our children, not add to their sorrow and wounding.

Offering forgiveness does not absolve what the person did or minimize the Event. It doesn't mean they got away with something. It also doesn't require us to engage with the person other than in matters concerning the children. It means that we let go of any expectation that those who wronged us owe us. If you lost your mate to a premature death, it means you forgive him (and anyone who may have caused his death) for leaving you and your children. There may be other people associated with the Event that we also have to forgive. We don't have to forgive in person, but we must forgive from the heart. If we're wise, we'll also include our self, acknowledging our own responsibility in the Event. It may be hard to face, but it is necessary. Why does Royalty offer a Pardon to certain subjects? The reasons are various according to the individual. But the main reason a King or Queen pardons someone is because... they CAN! That same kind of greatness lies within you and you must break any chains of unforgiveness that keep you from moving forward.

Offering forgiveness may be a process to work through and that's okay. I've learned on my journey of healing that forgiveness is complete when you can hold the offending person in your mind and say, "Thank you for-giving me this experience". It may be that the only thing you can be thankful for is your beautiful children, and that's enough. It's a sure sign that you are moving ahead.

We may not be able to control what the winds of life bring, but we can decide whether or not we will allow those winds to take from us. We have the power to decide and our answer should be a resounding... NO! We will not be defined or confined by any Event that tries to rob our greatness; alter our DNA. We will live in the full expression of all that we are meant to be and we will teach our children to do so. After all, we are Woman.

And so we have arrived at a crossroad located in the Valley of Decision. It is a place of choosing what you want for your self and your children. There are only two choices, so do so wisely. You can remain where you are or you can move forward into something new and beautiful. With gentleness and compassion I invite you to embark on a new journey; a path filled with discovery and wonder. It's a place where

> *We will live in the full expression of all that we are meant to be and we will teach our children to do so. After all, we are Woman.*

you can exchange your garments of yesterday for the regal robes of destiny and step into your rightful place of Greatness. It's your opportunity to come into agreement with your design as a Masterpiece and begin to live as one. Truly, it is, the only way...out.

Author's note: The following chapters will help you discover your Greatness by virtue of design. They do not contain information to assist with issues requiring emotional or inner healing.

Go Within or You'll Go Without

"I was always looking outside myself for strength and confidence, but it comes from within. It is there all the time."

Anna Freud ~ Austrian psychoanalyst & psychologist
(1895 -1982)

"Daughter"... "Sister"... "Aunt"... "Niece"... "Executive"... "Teacher"... "Associate"... "Neighbor"... "Girlfriend"... "Wife"... "Significant Other"... "Mother". From childhood to adulthood we've accumulated any number of labels or titles by which we are known. Some of these have been given to us and others are those we have made a part of our existence. These descriptions help those we interface with to recognize and identify us. Although these titles may be helpful to others in identifying our position, they don't adequately reveal our personhood. We may know that our neighbor, Jane, is a teacher who is married with three children and yet never discover who she is on the inside.

Sometimes we, ourselves, can become confused between what we do and who we are. If all our time is consumed with being a wife, mother and executive it can be very easy to lose touch with who we really are as a person. Now that most of our time is focused on Work, Kids, and Home it's very easy to feel like something is missing from our life and it is...it's you! Many single mothers tend to lose their own sense of self. For one thing, she is now without one of her titles ~ be it "wife" or "significant other". No longer is she engaging in the "love of His life" aspect of womanhood and this part of her now shifts from functional to dormant. This shift makes us feel different because we're not sharing a part of who we are and so it feels like something is missing. On the other hand, we are now in the mode of having to give so much of our time and our self to everyone and everything else. It's the epitome of "spreading yourself thin". Most single moms spread themselves "gone". Is it any wonder there seems to be a feeling of emptiness inside?

Society and its culture can also bring confusion to the equation of our personhood. Does it acknowledge a person for just "being" or does it reward for accomplishment? Are we accepted because of performance or are we accepted, period? Sometimes the standards are set very high and are almost impossible to attain no matter how hard we try. Because acceptance and belonging are so important to the majority, most people continue an attempt to scale the ladder of success erected by the standards of others who don't know us. If we fall into this trap, we then transform from human beings to human doings so we can "measure up". Everyone wants to be valued and accepted; it gives us a sense of belonging. But if we don't have a strong sense of who we are, we will succumb to the expectation and opinion of others who will then decide what we are worth.

From the beginning of time women have been tossed to and fro on the waves of the opinions of others. We have had to endure all kinds of stations in life because of outside influence. Even today in some parts of the world, women are told what their purpose and place is, and have been made to feel inferior by virtue of gender alone. But the real problem is not with what we are being told; it's the fact that **we have come into agreement with it!**

Because a majority of us do not know or understand our design of Greatness, we allow our worth to be shaped by the affirmation, validation and approval of others. We turn our power over to others when we give them our permission to determine our value. This is how we allow others to "rule" over us.

> *Until we go back and touch the home base of our genesis, we cannot go forward into the fullness of all we are meant to be.*

It's time to revisit our Master Design. We need to become well acquainted with our original DNA; therein reveals our Greatness. It is from this position that we will determine who we are and what makes us such a Masterpiece. We must return to our authentic self and come into full agreement with the truth that lives within; the truth that tells us who we really are. Until we go back and touch the home base of our genesis, we cannot go forward into the fullness of all we are meant to be.

Here's an incredible phrase I have learned (and am still learning) to incorporate into my life. I invite you to do the same:

Go Within or you'll Go Without

What this simple phrase is telling us is that everything you need is already inside you! The problem is that for too long we have looked to others for what we need and wonder why we continue to feel dissatisfied, empty and unfulfilled. We've taken on the identity, occupation, dreams, goals, vision, and ad infinitum of others only to shortchange our self in the equation [Go Without]. Is it any wonder why we feel frustrated and unhappy with life? The solution is to look inside, discover our authentic self and begin to live in **that** realm [Go Within]. Only then can we feel that we are living with purpose and destiny and that our lives have meaning. We will experience a true sense of fulfillment because indeed we are filled with the fullness of all we are meant to be. This is real living.

Everything we need is on the inside of us. You may find that hard to believe in your present situation, when finding a way out (through someone or something) seems like a never- ending quest. But believe me, it is nonetheless, true. Embrace this truth and your life will be forever changed and you will become your own unique Masterpiece.

At the very core of our existence, we are Woman.

Before we can discover our authentic self, we must shed the garments of yesterday and the ill-fitting apparel of today. Sometimes we have chosen the wrong clothing and other times friends and family have placed the wrong apparel on us. It's time to sort through our closet. This simple exercise will help you do just that. Take a piece of paper and write on it every descriptive word that was ever spoken about you, good or bad. I highly suggest you take at least a week or two to allow yourself to recall things you may have buried in your subconscious. Don't list Who said it, just the word or phrase. It's important you don't rush through this exercise; make sure your list is completed to the best of your ability. When you feel you have finished this list, it's time to sort.

Find a block of time where you can have absolute solitude. Take each word and say it out loud (as many times as you need). As you are hearing the word, take careful note of how it resonates within your Being. If your Being is not in full agreement with it, circle the word in red and put a line through it. If you are in agreement with the word, write it on a separate piece of paper. The words circled in red are descriptions that are not a part of your true self and should be discarded permanently. Be honest enough to include the descriptions that you personally have made a part of your wardrobe. I would suggest (carefully!) burning the piece of paper and offering forgiveness and release to those who were unable to discern your true self. You may also need to forgive your self in this process. Keep the list of words that do resonate with your authentic self and read them often. This will help you in discovering your "uniqueness" as you uncover your Greatness. Again, I highly suggest that you take your time and not rush through this process. Sorting through our self is not a quick and easy fix. Sometimes it's a struggle to get off a garment that doesn't fit well, but with patience and gentleness, it will be removed.

At this point we can begin to get a glimpse of our original design ~ Woman. In her unveiled form, she is beautiful in her essence alone. Her very Being exudes life and the ability to sustain it. Uniquely hers alone is the reality of being able to reproduce life within her self and pass on her DNA of Greatness. She is, indeed, the finishing touch of creation ~ a Masterpiece. She is …you!

To further understand this Greatness, we must return to the original intent and purpose for Woman. For this we must look once again to the original Prototype. Understanding the mission statement for Woman will help us understand our purpose and design and in this discovery, our Greatness.

" Produce, Increase, Subdue and Rule."

These words are powerful. Read them again, slowly and purposefully. As we look at them we may feel that our current state of Being is nowhere near comparison. But take heart my sister, my friend because even though you may not be functioning in this place of Greatness right now, your opportunity begins with your next breath. It's that close because it's written in the very fiber of your Being, it's your design. Now you can see why the answer to every need you have is within.

Go Within or you'll Go Without

The following pages will be a revelation, an unveiling, a discovery of Greatness...*your* Greatness. We will look at each aspect of who we are and how to walk in the fullness of all that we are.

Yes, we are single mothers, but first and foremost, we are Woman. In the difficulty of our present life circumstance we can call on the strength and Greatness of Woman for every need we have, for truly she lives...within.

Recapturing Your Authentic Self

The Unveiling

> *"I do not want to die... until I have faithfully made the most of my talent and cultivated the seed that was placed in me until the last small twig has grown."*
> Kathe Kollwitz, O Magazine, September 2002

For all the times we have come into agreement with the wrong words, labels, or descriptions about our self, we have before us a chance to make a complete turn around; a shift. It's time to fully embrace, align, and come into agreement with the Woman within. Only then are we able to move forward and live the life we were meant to live in all its fullness ~ living life from our Authentic Self.

Facets of the Greatness of Woman

Produce

At first glance we might think this word to be obvious and somewhat limiting. We may be tempted to declare, *"Produce? I have children!"* By physical design women are created to produce and bear children. For forty weeks our body becomes a sanctuary where a miracle is formed and fashioned. It really involves very little effort on our part. We go about our daily routine and all the while something incredible is happening on its own; Woman is creating a being in her image, inside herself. But there's more to this part of our design than bearing children.

In its truest meaning, Produce, is to:

bear fruit, bring forth, cause, make, grow, increase.[1]

Children are what we bring forth from our body, but this aspect of Produce also includes bringing forth that which is in our heart. It's from the place where our days of reverie in thought wrap themselves around a dream, a wish, a desire. It's where nothing becomes something because we give it permission to do so.

Being a single mother leaves us little time for our self, let alone any time to consider what is deep within the wells of our passion. All that seems so distant because our lives have become consumed with Have To. We're treading the choppy waters of life now and we're not quite sure we can let our heart dream again.

Life is so busy and if I had the time to just sit

and think, I would probably fall asleep!

We can come up with a multitude of reasons why we're not able to vocalize what is in our hearts. I would venture to say that the main reason is because we've haven't been there in a while. This is where we must purposefully choose to Go Within. This is a time to re-acquaint and reconnect. It's a time to revisit...Want To. This may feel very foreign and somewhat frightening to us because it may have been a very long time that we've even thought about Want To. Feelings of guilt may also arise as we take our focus off of everyone and everything else. If we're feeling uncomfortable about tending to our Self, it's a good sign that our life is out of balance. We need to invite those feelings to step aside because they will keep us from moving forward.

Think back to a time in your life when you dreamed of being or doing any thing you wanted. Nothing was impossible because you didn't know limitation. For many of us, that time existed in childhood. We gave a voice to our dreams by declaring, *"When I grow up, I'm going to be a ..."* or *"I'm going to..."* It was reverie at its best. Inside of us, lived a dream, desire or wish just waiting to get out. We gave our Self permission to daydream because at this stage in our life we were living from the heart. Today we are living from our heads. It's called Survival Mode. But the reason we have these thoughts in the first place is because it is programmed in our Design; it's how we were created.

For those who have and are living out the passion of their lives, I applaud you and invite you to take another look. There may be another dream or idea to birth. Don't pass it by because it may be something you consider "unimportant". If it's in your heart, it's important because it's a part of who you are. Others may not have been fortunate enough to discover their passion much less live it. The common denominator in all of us is that we have a heart that can dream, big or small, and others need what we have to bring forth.

> *Produce includes bringing forth that which is in our heart.*

Perhaps there is a cause living inside you. This cause is usually fueled by passion too. It can bring great benefits to the world in which we live. One cause, that hits close to home with mothers in general, created a group called MADD ~ Mothers Against Drunk Drivers. It was born out of the broken heart of a woman who lost her child to a drunk driver. Instead of living in bitterness and sorrow of heart, these women took on the courts and fought for laws to make Driving Under the Influence illegal. Their passion and cause changed the laws of an entire nation. Laws regarding child support have also changed because of women who took up a cause. We honor these women and their accomplishments. We honor their Woman.

So many women are creative and they have the ability to make something and/or make something happen. We all know women like this and we watch in amazement. We marvel and ask, *"How did you do that?"* Their reply, with equal amazement, is simply, *"Oh, it was nothing!"* These ladies have learned to tap into their natural talents and abilities, give permission and expression to them and make things/happen. It came from Within and found its way out.

As mothers we are, at times, astonished to see how fast our children grow (especially their feet!). *Didn't I just buy you a pair of shoes?* But the good news is, their bodies grow and develop on their own...it's one less thing we have to do! But we do help grow their character. We provide opportunities and life lessons as an arena for this to happen. While our children are a priority, there are other avenues where we can affect growth.

The list can be endless, but the principle constant. We can take something and give it whatever it needs to become more than what it was when we first became a part of it. It's taking it from Point A to Point B and being able to see a measurable change. Again, it's taking that which lies Within, engaging it with the opportunity before you and making a difference.

It seems that the busyness of our life supercedes any flame of passion that may exist in our heart. No question, it is the reality of our circumstances. It's not a requirement for you to "do" one more thing. It's having the understanding that you are able to produce what is in your heart, if and when you choose to do so. It eliminates the words, *I can't.* It takes the limits off our thinking because we now have learned that *I can because I am!* It's part of the Greatness of our DNA.

Increase

First glance at this word and most single mothers think of finances. It's a rarity to meet a single mom who couldn't use more resources. Increase has a multitude of meanings that are sure to bring you hope.

It means to:
1. increase in whatever respect
2. bring in abundance
3. enlarge, excell
4. be full of, make great
5. be in authority
6. multiply and continue to do so
7. be more in number
8. nourish
9. have plenty, overflow[2]

For many single mothers this list seems almost too impossible to believe. The words that describe our situation are more like ~ scarce, lack, sparse, insufficient, stretched, broke, short, etc. But looking through this list, keep in mind that, Increase is a facet of who we are as Woman.

How wonderful that Increase is not limited to finances alone! The first definition says we can increase in whatever respect. Wow! As single mothers there are a lot of things we could use. How about wisdom? Raising children on our own requires wisdom! In the area of finances we can use (a lot of) wisdom. How to continue a (normal) family life, planning for the children's' future, and re-creating our life after the children leave home are major areas where wisdom is desperately needed. What about time? Is it possible that time could also be included in the "whatever respect" of Increase? How about peace, favor, hope, creativity, position, skills, vision? A single mother needs all of these things to help her move forward.

I know it sounds too good to be true when you feel like life is one big struggle, but it is nonetheless, a part of your Greatness. And again, I remind you, that this is not something that you are trying to attain. Increase is a facet of how you already are designed to function.

> *Increase is a facet of how you already are designed to function.*

I would like to challenge you with the following

THE UNVEILING • 79

exercise. Get a notebook and write each of these definitions at the top of its own page. As you learn to come into agreement with the facet of Increase in your life, write down how you have subsequently experienced Increase. You may or may not have something written under every definition and that's perfectly okay. Again, it's not about doing, it's about Being. Taking note of Increase on these pages will reveal how much of your Within is being released. There's no pressure and no timeline. Think of it as a "growth chart". You might want to add the date to show the progress you have made. Below are a few examples:

A. Enlarge
Came into greater understanding of the DNA of my Greatness. Recognized limiting beliefs I have carried for years. Expanded my thinking.
~ April 12th

B. Excel
Received the best job evaluation I've ever had!
~ August 8th

C. Bring in Abundance
Thought of how I can turn the skills I already have into a side business.
 ~ October 21st

D. Have plenty, Overflow
Went through some emotional healing and restoration. Now I have more love to give to my children.
~ November 10th

Increase is an incredible facet of Woman because it encompasses every area of our life that we want it to; it's without limits! We get to choose how to form and fashion it into the tapestry of our Being however we desire. We must purpose in our heart to break off the constraints we feel imposed on us by the circumstances of our current situation. The only limitation to Increase is our thinking! Are you ready to break out and break forth?

Endnotes

1. James Strong, The New Strong's Exhaustive Concordance of the Bible,
   (Nashville: Thomas Nelson Publishers, 1990) Old Testament section 6509.
2. James Strong, The New Strong's Exhaustive Concordance of the Bible,
   (Nashville: Thomas Nelson Publisher, 1990) Old Testament section 7235.

   note: All endnote references are utilized with the author's license to paraphrase. You are encouraged to research the above references for your own study purposes.

9
More Revelation

"The key to realizing a dream is to focus not on success but significance - and then even the small steps and little victories along your path will take on greater meaning."
Oprah Winfrey (1954 -)

After reading the previous chapter you may be thinking, *"Is this for real? Surely this lady doesn't mean ME because I don't look like the Woman she's talking about at all!"* That's okay! We're all in the process of evolving and discovering who we are as Woman. The good news is that we now have before us a template, model and picture of our true Design. She in us and we in Her. She/we have so much to offer!

Subdue

First glance at the word Subdue and what comes to mind is some type of conflict in which one needs to exert power. It speaks of a struggle or contest of wills where there is a use of force.

Subdue also implies an outcome where someone wins and someone loses. Certainly one would come to such a conclusion when discovering the definition of Subdue is:

>to tread down, conquer, subjugate, to force, to bring into bondage or subjection.[1]

Reduced to its simplest terms the word Subdue evokes the feeling of more stress, trouble and a high expenditure of energy to a single mother. *Don't I have enough to deal with already? I don't think I'm interested in this facet of Woman!* We're going to take a closer look at the word Subdue and I assure you, you will be delightfully surprised!

At face value, the literal definition of the word Subdue does appear to be that of aggression. But upon further study, we find another element that sheds a whole different light on its true meaning. What we need to really comprehend about this word is the tone, mood, feeling and intention behind it. The emotion and intention wrapped around the definition is not about power, force and conflict. Rather, it is completely the opposite!

The truest intention of Subdue is to entice or to woo. It also speaks of entreating and inviting. Its desire is to bring to fullness of purpose the individual, circumstance or situation before us.[2] The motive behind the action is, without a doubt, pure. Its focus is on the benefit and good of all involved.

As mothers we may have done this without really being aware of it!

A wonderful example of this is helping our newborn to suckle. There are times when a newborn may not possess a strong sucking reflex. New mothers are quick to discover that forcing and getting upset with the child does nothing more than produce a bigger problem and a crying baby that refuses to nurse or take a bottle! This is where an experienced mother knows how to Subdue the little one with wisdom. She has learned (probably from another mother!) to take the pad of her finger and gently stimulate the palate of the newborn. This gentle motion helps the newborn learn to suckle. Once the reflex is stimulated the baby then learns what to do with the breast or bottle and receives nourishment. The outcome has produced a win-win solution. Mission accomplished and everyone is happy! What a beautiful example of the word Subdue.

When we don't know how to operate in the pure realm of Subduing, many women resort to its counterfeit, which in all reality is its perversion. It's called "manipulation". Manipulation is where we try to produce a desired outcome for our own benefit. We maneuver and handle people, situations and circumstances so that we get what we want. Women are incredibly gifted at manipulation and some women have even learned to "work it" to an exact science! But here's the difference. No one wins! Oh sure, you may get what you want, but it's not truly fulfilling and leaves you with an empty feeling, if you are really honest about it. Why? Because the person or situation turned in your favor by the issue of force and not from the heart. It sure feels a whole lot different when something turns in our favor because it was meant to or someone does something for us because they genuinely want to. There is a peace and joy produced with this outcome, along with a real sense of fulfillment.

> *The strength we possess within can find its true expression in our ability to Subdue.*

Why are we so good at manipulation? Because, we don't know the truth of what we possess on the inside. When left to our own knowledge or devices, some of us have followed the faulty pattern that we've been exposed to. No one may have told us there is another way. We may not have learned that this part of Woman lives in our DNA and this is another aspect that contributes to our Greatness.

We don't have to live beneath what we truly are to bring about what we really want. We are a Woman of Greatness; we can release what we live on the inside to produce a desired end. The strength we possess within can find its true expression in our ability to Subdue when we remember to focus on the fulfillment of purpose.

Rule

The cool wind coming through my window was fragrant with the smell of stately pine trees that stood majestically along the winding mountain road. Here I was in paradise...at least my idea of paradise! A much-needed get-away weekend was in order for this very tired single mom. A couple days of rest and relaxation always does wonders for the body, but it also does miracles for the soul. I could let go of all the weight of the responsibility that rested so heavily upon my shoulders... if only for two days. But that particular reprieve brought an unexpected surprise. Being surrounded by such magnificent beauty gave peace the opportunity to quiet the thoughts that continuously raced in my mind. It was in this place of solitude and serenity that I had an epiphany of sorts ~ a revelation, illumination, a shift. Coming from deep inside my Being I heard these words,

"I'm not supposed to be dominated by life, I'm supposed to have dominion."

The truth of what I knew in my heart was overcome by the condition and state of life in which I was living. I was being dominated by single motherhood and the struggle to survive. Because I didn't have a full understanding of this truth, I came to realize that I was "standing under" the circumstances of my life. Is it any wonder we feel so much pressure?

That day was pivotal for me; the shift in my thinking began the shift in my life. Step by step I began to walk out "from under". The correlation was obvious. As I changed my thoughts, I changed my circumstances. And the answer came from within! The process has taken some time and effort, but it was well worth my energy. Even today I continue to evolve in this area and aspect of Woman. It's time for your shift.

As single mothers we certainly have felt dominated by our circumstances. It may seem unthinkable that we were created to have dominion ~ to Rule. But this is where we shift our thinking once more. And what exactly does is mean to Rule anyway? Primarily the word denotes:

reigning, prevail against, tread down, rule over, come to have dominion. [3]

It may be the exact opposite of where you are positioned in life right now. You may feel that you also are living "from under". Gaining understanding about what it means to Rule will shift you from under to over. Your days of being dominated by life can finally begin to fade away.

Perhaps the word Rule has a negative connotation in your thought process. Your history may contain unpleasant memories of someone who has ruled over you. That alone can turn you away from this aspect of Woman. But this is not about exertion of perverse power. This facet has no connection to ruling with an iron fist but rather reveals a strength that flows from the heart.

Rule conveys leadership in its highest and purest form. William Ross Wallace gave great insight to the meaning of Rule with the following quote:

"The hand that rocks the cradle rules the world."

Do we really equate Motherhood with leadership? Can we actually perceive the importance of our role in shaping the life of another human being? Do we have a thorough understanding that we are creating the culture and society of tomorrow? Despite the difficult circumstances we presently find ourselves in, we must fully comprehend that our children are in desperate need of solid leadership. Can they look to us for stability, security and strength? Will we pass up the opportunity or pass down the Greatness? Legacy is a gift we have to pass onward.

This concept of Rule also conveys influence. How well we understand the power of influence with regard to our children! We know that whatever has an influence over them can have a profound and lasting affect on their lives. This is where our leadership steps in and if we have to tread down or prevail against anything that would try to bring destruction to our children, we will. What we want for our children is a strong and positive example to emulate and it should begin with us. A popular truism with children is that "more is caught than is taught". What they observe from watching us should be a demonstration on how to Rule in life.

You may think that your place of leadership and sphere of influence is solely confined to Motherhood. Think again! You will impact every person, association and relationship in your life. What strength do you have to offer? How can you make a difference in the lives of those around you? The Greatness inside of you needs to be broken into the lives of others. People need what you have. What do you have to give?

> *Realigning our self in the proper position gives us the momentum to move forward.*

Woman was designed to Rule and that implies having power. It's a place of prevailing in whatever situation we find ourselves. Certainly single motherhood is tough at best, but we can choose not to "live under" our circumstances even if they don't change. We don't have to view ourselves as powerless victims but rather we can choose to define ourselves by Who we are within. Aligning ourselves with this power to Rule allows us to shift from under to over. Re-aligning our self in the proper position gives us the momentum to move forward.

It's time to make your move...to Within.

Endnotes

1. James Strong, The New Strong's Exhaustive Concordance of the Bible,
   (Nashville: Thomas Nelson Publishers, 1990), Old Testament section 3533.
2. The Exegeses Ready Research Bible KJV, Herb Jahn exegete, World Bible Publishers, Iowa Falls, IA 50126, 1992.
   Gesenius' Hebrew-Chaldee Lexicon to the Old Testament, H.W.F. Gesenius,
   Baker Book House, Grand Rapids, MI, 1979.
3. James Strong, The New Strong's Exhaustive Concordance of the Bible,
   (Nashville: Thomas Nelson Publishers, 1990), Old Testament section 7287.

   note: All endnote references are utilized with the author's license to paraphrase. You are encouraged to research the above references for your own study purposes.

10
Practically Speaking

> *"And now here is my secret, a very simple secret; it is only with the heart that one can see rightly, what is essential is invisible to the eye."*
> Antoine de Saint-Exupery

We have completed our journey through a very real, sacred and living temple ~ Woman and her Authentic Self. We've taken a glimpse into her inner workings to see her magnificence and Greatness. We've observed the hidden beauty and power that live within the foundation of her Being. We have viewed her up close and personally and we are amazed at who she is. And though there is much we have discovered about her, there's so much more she has to reveal. Woman is like a diamond; each facet she displays radiates its own incredible brilliance and beauty. Truly, Woman is the "finishing touch" of creation.

Soundness, wholeness, and completeness are the gifts she brings with her.

She is not someone that we envy or aspire to be like. The pressure to compete with Her is nonexistent and the yardstick of comparison is nowhere to be found. She comes to us in the opposite spirit and her greeting is one of peace; nothing lacking, nothing missing. Soundness, wholeness, and completeness are the gifts she brings with her. As she comes close enough to greet us face to face, a light shines forth from her eyes. It's a light of reflection and of deep calling unto deep. Looking into her eyes we see a reflection of...our Self; the template, prototype and original divine Design. She lives in us; she is us. At the very core of our existence, we are Woman.

That thought may take some getting used to. The mind-sets and strongholds of our self-image may not allow us to accept and embrace this truth in this moment. Our physical image confirms our gender as Woman, but we may be lacking a conscious acknowledgment of all the Facets we learned about.

"Are you kidding? I don't resemble her at all!

"You must be talking about someone else because if you knew me, you would know I'm nothing like her."

"She may be that wonderful but I'm certainly not! I don't even come close."

"This is too good to be true, but if she did live in me, HOW IN THE WORLD DO I LET HER OUT?"

The key to walking in the fullness of who we are as Woman is to first and foremost be single-minded about Her image that lives is us. If we are not single-minded about our image, then we will live beneath all we are meant to be. Some of us have lived there long enough and we're ready to shift from living beneath to living above! So, what does it mean to be single-minded? To help us understand this concept, let's first look at what it isn't.

Being single-minded doesn't mean that we aren't swayed between various thoughts while desperately trying to fixate on the primary concept. It also doesn't mean that we can't change our mind, incorporate new information or question our primary beliefs. Many people think that being single-minded is the ability to concentrate and maintain focus that is limited to one thing and one thing only. Untrue! It goes much deeper than that!

Single-mindedness involves not only our thoughts but also our heart! It means that what we believe in our mind is the same thing we feel in our heart. There is a congruence or agreement, if you will, between the two. There is a tremendous connection between the heart and the mind. The two must be in unison for our lives to be fruitful. If they are in conflict or disagreement, the feelings of the heart will always win. But here's the problem. Most people truly think they know what they believe. They will tell themselves over and over again what they believe, but their life doesn't reflect their beliefs. Why? Because, they are not single-minded.

I can't tell you how many "positive thinking" books I've read over the years. Each one makes a promise that wonderful things will occur if all you do is maintain a positive focus. It all sounded so simple and since I'm generally a positive person, success seemed imminent! I followed each step, recited every affirmation and kept my focus with all the strength I had. I put a lot of time and effort into this practice because there were so many stories of people whose lives had changed dramatically using this tool. I was ready for change in my life too! Much to my dismay, it never "worked". How was that possible since I really believed in what I was saying? The truth is, I wasn't single-minded. I was double-minded; my mind thought one thing and my heart felt the opposite. How come those books didn't tell me about this very important detail? Why didn't they teach me that it I could unknowingly sabotage my own efforts! For many years I fought against myself and went NOWHERE! Until I learned how to be single-minded my life never changed.

Now to answer the obvious question...*How do I know if I'm single-minded?*

It's very easy! Our physical body is the umpire and can discern between the true and the false. The body is a phenomenal machine and has some incredible qualities. One of its attributes is that it cannot lie! Think of a polygraph test. When a person answers a question untruthfully, the body responds and it shows up on a polygraph test. Don't worry; you don't have to purchase a machine to help you determine if you are single or double-minded, a simple muscle test will do. Here's a great method for beginners: (Enlist the help a friend or one of your kids.) Hold your arm out to the side at shoulder level. Say your name out loud ~ *My name is...* and then have your assistant push your arm down while you resist. You should remain strong because you're telling the truth. Do the same test again using a different name and you will go weak. (It doesn't require a lot of force to test.) Your body will react because the truth you know in your heart (your real name) is different from what your mind is declaring (a false name). An amazing fact about this testing is that you don't even have to say it out loud!

Using this tool is wonderful to determine single-mindedness. Suppose you want a better job but no matter how many interviews you go on, you never seem to get the position. Try muscle testing to see if you are "in agreement" with yourself!

First test what you think, then test what you feel. Example:

I think I deserve a better job (muscle test).
I feel I deserve a better job (muscle test).

If you go weak on what you "feel" then you need to realize this is what you truly believe. How would this prevent you from getting a better job? Our subconscious has its own form of non-verbal communication and it will speak during your interview! It will convey what you really believe and your interviewer will detect it. It's all done on a subconscious level, but it speaks loudly!

By the way, this technique works great on your kids! *Where did you say you went with your friends?* (Muscle test the answer!)

So why is all this "single-mindedness" so important? It goes right back to what I've been saying all through this book...

We cannot go through a life-altering event and not come out unaffected.

If we don't deal with the issues of our heart, we will stay imprinted by every Event that happens in our life and that can cause us to be double-minded. It can also lead to misperceptions, false beliefs, mindsets and strongholds in our thinking that leads to self-limitation, which keeps us cemented in our circumstances.

This is why we must become responsible for our Self; it's the only way to truly make progress in our difficult circumstances and move forward.

I can hear your next question because I've asked it myself!

How do I change those limiting beliefs in my heart and embrace the Woman in me?

It really involves a two-part process that happens simultaneously. The first part is to come into agreement and embrace the Woman within. The second part is that you need to be actively working on inner healing; deal with your issues. Think of planting a new floral garden. You go to the local nursery and pick out the most beautiful flowers and bring them home ready to plant. But once you get them home, you realize you need to tend the ground where you want to plant them. The process begins of turning the soil, pulling grass or weeds, discarding rocks, sticks and other debris. Then you add some topsoil to nourish the new plantings. Though this is not a fun activity, every glance at the flowers gives you the desire to continue the job so you can enjoy a beautiful garden.

> *At the very core of our existence, we are Woman.*

After the flowers are planted, you still have to tend the garden ~ pull weeds, spray for bugs, watch for disease, etc. The same is true for our heart. Remember, "self talk"? This is a particularly important conversation to be tuned into because it's your heart speaking! You will certainly "locate" yourself by listening to your Self, talk. Here's another clue you need to pay attention to. Any time you don't feel at peace, you need to Go Within. Tending the garden of your heart is of utmost importance to continually and successfully, move you forward into a brighter future. Coming into agreement and embracing Woman is really quite simple. The easiest way is to re-read chapters 8 and 9 and study her Facets... **your** facets. These Facets are the flowers that already live in the garden of your heart ~ a beautiful bouquet presented at your birth. You came equipped with this glorious floral arrangement but didn't recognize it because you weren't told it was there or it became covered over by the Events that had happened up to thispoint. Let me show you in a practical sense how this works.

> *Tending the garden of your heart is important to continually and successfully move you forward.*

During my pregnancy, I, along with most mothers, looked through numerous books of baby names. Not knowing the gender of my child, I carefully contemplated a name for a boy and girl. My focus was not on something fashionable or chic, nor did I want to name the baby after a special relative. I wanted a name that described what I wanted my child to become. After the birth of my son, he was named Brian Matthew. Brian means, "strength, honor" and Matthew means, "gift of

God". During his growing up years we would often talk about what his name meant. I also told him he was a leader and that he had so many talents to share with others. Sometimes, instead of calling him by "Brian", I would say "strength and honor!"… "gift of God!". This was a way to reveal <u>his</u> bouquet, if you will. When he behaved in a way that needed correction I would, at times, handle it this way:

Tell me your name.
Brian.
What does your name mean?
Strength and honor.
Was there any strength or honor in what you just did?
No.
Is that what a leader does?
No.
*Then you can't do that because that's not who you are. Now, be who you **are.***

Telling him who he is gave him a roadmap to pattern his life after. I am grateful to say that Brian, now in his early 20s, is a young man that I genuinely admire. Not solely because he's my son, but because I observe strength, honor and leadership in his life.

Because we weren't told who we are, we now have to tell our Self. This is how we embrace the

Greatness we have as Woman. She in us and we in her. Add to that the unique personality and strengths we also possess and you can see why we have so much to offer!

> *"Life"... "Breath"... "Living One"... "Mother"... "Woman".*

Begin to tell yourself who you really are, what you actually have and how much you have to offer. Start living from the inside…out! Enjoy all the beauty that you possess and then pass this onto your children and other women. This surely is the only way out!

She comes to us in the opposite spirit and her greeting is one of peace ~ nothing lacking, nothing missing. Soundness, wholeness, and completeness are the gifts she brings with her. As she comes close enough to greet us face to face, a light shines forth from her eyes. It's a light of reflection and of deep calling unto deep. Looking into her eyes we see a reflection of…our Self; the template, prototype and original divine Design. She lives in us; she is us. At the very core of our existence, we are Woman.

My sister, my friend, this is who we truly are: a design of Greatness, a Masterpiece of creation, a multi-faceted diamond of exquisite beauty ~ complete within ~ nothing lacking, nothing missing.

For those of you who have never been presented with your own beautiful bouquet, I extend my hand of grace and offer you a gift of truth today. May the garden of your heart be the setting where Woman lives and flourishes…abundantly.

LaVergne, TN USA
19 December 2009
167604LV00001B/3/P